"Pray without ceasing." 1 Thessalonians 5:17

ISBN-13: 979-8-88870-226-0 (paperback specially made for James)

En Route Books and Media, LLC
5705 Rhodes Avenue
St. Louis, MO 63109

Contact us at contactus@enroutebooksandmedia.com

I Talk to God About You

Sr. M. Gianna Casino   Yuna Chan

I talk to God
about you,
each and
every day.

From the moment
I first saw you,
my heart moved me
to pray.

I pray for you
as you sleep,
and when
you're wide awake.

I pray that you will feel
God's love,
after a mistake.

I pray for you on days
that are good,
and on days that can
seem bad.

I pray for you
when you feel scared,
and at times
when you feel sad.

I tell God
what my *dreams*
are for you,
and wonder
what you will achieve.

I pray He gives you
all the strength,
to love
what you *believe.*

I *wonder* what
the plan of God
holds for you
to see.

Maybe you will
fly to space, or
sail the deep blue sea.

With God,
you can do
little things,
with a lot of *love.*

With God, you can do
great big things,
as He *blesses* you
above.

Wherever you are and
whatever you do,
I'm with you in prayer
and I'll always love you.

Good night, my little one.
Tomorrow, the sun will rise.

Would you like to pray with me,
before you close your eyes?

Let's Pray

Pray together as a family!
Jesus says,
"For where two or three are gathered in my name,
there am I in the midst of them" (Mt 18:20).

What do you want to tell God?

What do you want to thank God for?

What do you want to ask God?

Listen to God in silence.

What is He saying to you?

Can you spot Mother Mary in the story?

Mary is the Mother of Jesus, and your Mother too!
Mary is always with us.

The Kitchen Madonna

Our Lady of Guadalupe

Can you spot the saints?

Do you see St. Gianna Beretta Molla?

In less than 40 years, Gianna became an Italian wife, mother, pediatrician, and saint! A pediatrician is a special doctor who takes care of children. Gianna and her husband Pietro Molla, were blessed with three children. One day, Gianna found out she would have another baby, but something happened. The doctors told Gianna that having the baby meant she could become very sick and her life would be in danger. Gianna decided she wanted to have the baby anyway, because she loved her baby so much. Dr. Gianna's heroic choice and sacrifice enabled her youngest child, Gianna Emanuela, to be born. Pope St. John Paul II canonized Gianna Beretta Molla in 2004, and her husband and children were all at the ceremony. Look at the story. Do you see her youngest baby, Gianna Emanuela Molla? Do you see Pietro, the husband of St. Gianna?
St. Gianna Beretta Molla, pray for us!

Do you see a young Pope St. John Paul II?

Pope John Paul II was born in Poland as Karol Józef Wojtyla (his birth name). He had a big heart and a big smile that made everyone around him happy. Karol enjoyed playing soccer with his older brother. He loved assisting the priest at Church. He was also an outstanding student and a talented actor. Karol loved the Blessed Virgin Mary with all his heart and prayed the rosary daily. Losing his parents and his brother at an early age was a heavy cross to bear. He studied to become a priest and inspired millions of people. Throughout his years as pope, he visited 129 countries. Pope St. John Paul II's parents were both proclaimed Servants of God. Do you see the future pope with his mom, Emilia Wojtyla?
Pope St. John Paul II, pray for us!

Do you see a young St. Therese of Lisieux?

People lovingly call St. Therese, "The Little Flower." St. Therese did all things, big and small - even the tiniest- with a lot of love. Her way became known as "the little way," a short and straight way to Heaven. As a little girl, Therese had great faith. When she was four, her mother passed away, but Therese always remembered her mother's love. Therese had four other sisters. They all became nuns! At 15, Therese felt Jesus calling her to also become a nun. She went to live in a special place called a convent and devoted her whole life to Jesus. St. Therese continues to touch people's hearts all over the world, reminding us that even the smallest acts of love can have the biggest impact. Her parents, St. Louis and St. Zelie Martin, were the first married couple to ever be canonized (recognized as Saints) in the Church.

St. Therese of Lisieux, pray for us!

Do you see a young Venerable Augustus Tolton?

In 1886, Venerable Augustus Tolton became the first black Roman Catholic priest in America. John Augustus Tolton was born into slavery. Augustus and his mother were baptized as Catholics and escaped slavery by crossing the Mississippi River. Upon freedom, his mom turned to him and said, "John, boy, you're free. Never forget the goodness of the Lord." John Augustus never forgot God's goodness. He felt God calling him to the priesthood, but no American seminary would accept him because of the color of his skin. Augustus didn't give up! With his friend Fr. McGirr cheering him on, Augustus studied at a seminary and was ordained in Rome. Father Tolton learned to speak English, German, Italian, African dialects, Latin, and Greek. He was also a talented musician with an incredible voice.

Venerable Augustus Tolton, pray for us!

Saints are holy men and women in Heaven.
You are called to become a great saint too!

Do you see a young St. Giuseppe Moscati?

Giuseppe was a kind, caring doctor and scientist who lived in Italy. He attended the University of Naples and proclaimed his faith there when others were against it. Giuseppe became a researcher, medical professor, and pioneer in biochemistry. As he cared for the sick, Giuseppe always had a smile on his face. Whether his patients were poor or rich, he showed everyone the same compassion. When the volcano Mount Vesuvius erupted, Dr. Giuseppe rescued many patients out of the hospital and saved their lives. Giuseppe attended mass every day throughout his life. He was the first person to introduce insulin therapy to Italy. In 1987, Pope St. John Paul II canonized him.
St. Giuseppe Moscati, pray for us!

Do you see a young St. Teresa of Calcutta?

Mother Teresa was a Catholic Missionary Sister who loved the Sacred Heart of Jesus. She did little things with great love. She developed a great love for souls after receiving her First Communion at five and a half years old. Her father passed away suddenly when she was eight years old, and she was inspired by the way that her mother provided for everyone. At eighteen, she joined the Sisters of Loreto and became a missionary sister. Moved to love Jesus by caring for the sick and the poor, Mother Teresa established the Missionaries of Charity. She visited families in the slums and cared for the sick and dying who lay on the road. She opened homes for them, and her mission houses expanded worldwide. Mother Teresa won the Nobel Peace Prize in 1979. Many people loved her. Presidents, queens, people of all religions, the poor and the rich, were all present at her funeral. To this day, her missionary sisters care for people all over the world!
St. Teresa of Calcutta, pray for us!

Do you see a young St. John Bosco?

St. John Bosco is the patron saint of youth, publishers, and performers. As a young boy, John loved watching circus shows and taught himself tricks and acrobatics. He gathered his friends to put on little shows where he would juggle, walk a tightrope, tell stories, and pray with them. His admission required one rosary to be recited by audience members. The show grounds were in front of the house, where his mother often watched him. After his father passed away, John's childhood was marked with hardship, but he grew to have a big heart. John Bosco became a priest and cared for poor boys in Turin. He created a special place called an Oratory where these boys could learn, have fun, and receive religious instruction. Fr. John founded the Society of St. Francis de Sales, known as the Salesians. He also founded a congregation with St. Mary Mazzarello, known today as the Salesian Sisters.

St. John Bosco, pray for us!

Do you see a young St. Pedro Calungsod?

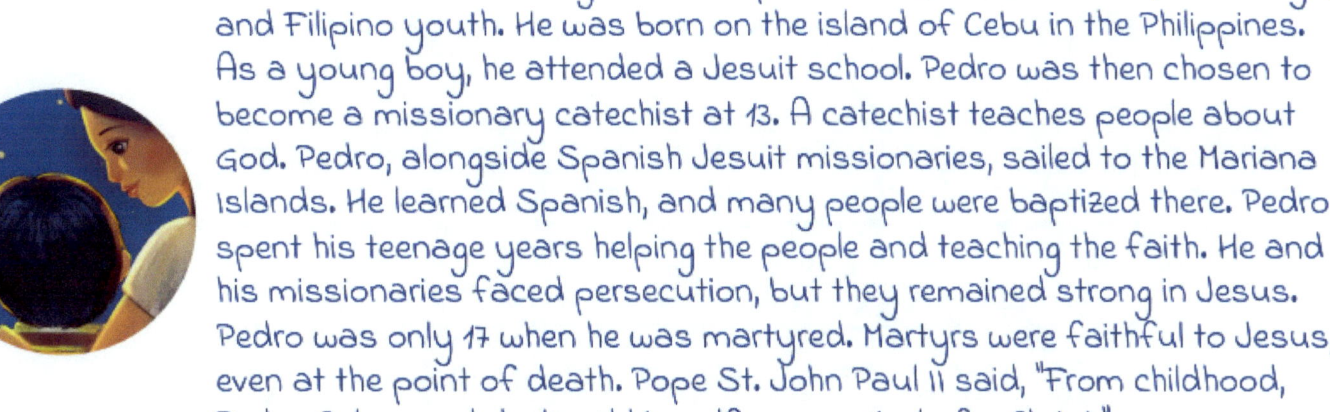

St. Pedro Calungsod is the patron saint of catechists, altar boys, and Filipino youth. He was born on the island of Cebu in the Philippines. As a young boy, he attended a Jesuit school. Pedro was then chosen to become a missionary catechist at 13. A catechist teaches people about God. Pedro, alongside Spanish Jesuit missionaries, sailed to the Mariana Islands. He learned Spanish, and many people were baptized there. Pedro spent his teenage years helping the people and teaching the faith. He and his missionaries faced persecution, but they remained strong in Jesus. Pedro was only 17 when he was martyred. Martyrs were faithful to Jesus, even at the point of death. Pope St. John Paul II said, "From childhood, Pedro Calungsod declared himself unwaveringly for Christ."

St. Pedro Calungsod, pray for us!

James,
become a saint!

This book was especially made for:

____

Wherever you are and whatever you do,
I am with you in prayer and I'll always love you.

____

If you enjoyed this book and want more activities,
scan the QR code below!

A Note to Author on her patronness, prayer, and
I Talk to God About You

Dear Sister Gianna,

Thank you so very much for your email, the picture, and, above all, for being named in honor of my Saint Mom, St. Gianna Beretta Molla!

My Parents, for my siblings and I, have been Mom and Dad for 48 years, almost half a century! Both of them totally sacrificed their lives for us, the children, in different ways. Even though Mom and Dad were thousands of kilometers apart, they were in fact deeply close to each other, thanks to the immense love which united them, and to their very intense, mutual prayer.

Thank you so very much, in honor of my Saint Mom and holy Dad!

God bless you,

Gianna Emanuela

Dr. Gianna Emanuela Molla and her father, Pietro Molla, meet St. John Paul II in 2004. It was the first time a husband witnessed his wife's canonization. (CNS photo/Andrew Hansen, courtesy Diocese of Springfield)